Lost in the Hills

Petra Pierre-Robertson

Bamboo Talk Press

Copyright © 2019 Petra Pierre-Robertson

All rights reserved. No portion of this book may be reproduced in any form or by any means, electronic or mechanical, including photocopying and recording, or by any information storage or retrieval system without the written permission of the author.

ISBN 9781097439188

Published by Bamboo Talk Press
Cover Design by Clive Strachan
Printed in Trinidad and Tobago

Bamboo Talk Press
Trinidad
www.bambootalkpress.org

Dedication

After the hike we joked among ourselves saying, "This is a good story to tell our children and our grandchildren in years to come!" The years flew. The time has come.

To Jean-Luc, here is the story.

To the group of fifteen; Delano Henry, Henry Woods, Petra Pierre, Frankie Hall, Janice McLean, Eric Pompey, Dawn Cameron, Yvette Regis - Pierre, Judith Murrell, Hazel Ann Edwards, Michelle Danglad, Cheryl Sharp, Shelly Barzey, Wendy McKenzie, Jocelyn Pierre.

To the memory of Janice McLean, a part of the fifteen who, unbelievably, is now gone but certainly not forgotten.

Acknowledgement

God for the ongoing inspiration

Clive Strachan for the layout and design

Paula Obe of Bamboo Talk Press

DL Robertson for the constant encouragement

Lystra Allicock for editing

Delano for the constant reminder that this publication

was long overdue

Foreword

Lost in the Hills is more than just an adventure story. Although targeted to teens, youth and young adults, it is an easy, interesting and riveting read for children and seniors. It is not restricted to either gender or geographic domain. Set in the hills of Trinidad, the themes explored may be applied in any context. The major theme running through the thread of the narrative is the importance of advance planning and the avoidance of shortcuts. It is told in the third person narrative voice by Peach, the main protagonist who easily captures the local dialect in her interactions with the other characters. In typical fashion Pierre - Robertson employs rich dialogue in capturing the realness of the sights, sounds and language of the Caribbean. She keeps the reader riveted as she moves the plot swiftly along. I highly recommend this narrative as a gripping and pleasurable read not just for Pathfinders but for the entire family.

Dr. Clive Dottin, Field Secretary Caribbean Union Conference

From the Author

Lost in the hills is an adventure story for the entire family. Although based on an actual occurrence, descriptions, depictions and dialogues have been enhanced to capture the language, sounds, sights and settings of the Caribbean, as well as to weave Pathfinder skills into the plot. Skills such as knot tying, first aid, purifying water, stargazing and hiking are subtly explored during the recounting of the experience. In addition, the story also shows the importance of resilience, patience, avoiding shortcuts and God's longsuffering and protection, despite our shortcomings that may lead to things going wrong. It imperceptibly hints to young leaders, the importance of following policy and procedure when placed in positions of authority.

Petra Pierre – Robertson

Author

Lost in the Hills

Chapter 1 – Our Orienteering Honor

The sun was still slowly making its way up the peak of the mountains encircling her home, yet Peach was uncharacteristically up. She yawned and stretched lazily. Skinny arms created a faint shadow on the wall that resembled a dried up tree branch. She giggled at the awkward caricature her slender frame engendered before returning her attention longingly to her pillow and blanket. She wanted to crawl back under the blanket, roll over, clutch her pillow to her chest, shut her eyes and just drift back into that lovely dream she was having before her mind alerted her body of the need to rise early. Mornings were not her favorite time of day by any stretch of the imagination. *Drat. That requirement for the Pathfinder Guide Class that had her getting up before the sun: to track a trail through unfamiliar territory, using just a map and a compass; the practical requirement for*

Lost in the Hills

the pathfinder orienteering honor. She sighed and sat up on the bed even as it begged her, "Peach, don't leave me."

Why did they have to do this on a Sunday; her favorite day to sleep late? Weekdays were so crazy! Apart from school, she found herself constantly running from one church activity to the next - drama, basketball, choir practice, club meeting, district meeting and don't forget midweek church meetings. This particular Sunday had been earmarked for sleeping late and lazing; something she had not been able to do for weeks.

The hike was not a planned event; well not in the truest sense of the word. The club was in the final stages of the completion of the honor necessary for them to acquire the Guide pin, in time for National Investiture which was less than a month away. There was just one activity they needed to do to complete the requirement - the difficult and mentally consuming Orienteering honor. The requirement was simple enough - *Prove your ability in the use of a map and/or a compass by following a one-mile (1.6 km) cross-country course with at least five given readings or control points.* Considering those variables, who could blame the group of fourteen for slipping discreetly out of Adventist Youth meeting at the stroke of sunset to head to the youth hall, to urgently plan a quick expedition? They did not all leave at the same time. One by one they slipped out. The Adventist Youth leader was in the process of announcing the closing song and prayer anyway. As they converged in the hall, the strains of the closing song floated up to them from the main church auditorium.

"Ok, people, I have the maps and compasses. Those who did not pay for a compass do so now before collecting. No one will be making this trip with me without a compass." Doug's no nonsense tone and stern face normally evoked the obedience required when he chose to use them to his advantage. Slim and lean, his training in the military made him appear sterner than he actually was. He was also one of the senior volunteer instructors

Lost in the Hills

with the Conference, with special focus on outdoor skills, drilling and marching. Brown-skinned with sharp, angular features, he was feared by his charges. Those close to him, however, were witnesses to an alternative jovial personality which presented itself only at select moments. Hands dug into pockets. The majority had not paid in advance as had been required. No one wanted to face Doug's chastisement.

"The trail is a short one. I did not get a chance to check it out recently but it is a simple enough trail."

"What about church board consent?" Peach questioned. Appearing too young for the position of Assistant Master Guide Leader, Peach was actually a product of AJY and Pathfinders. She had been placed in leadership positions in the church from as early as thirteen years when she was first appointed Sabbath School Secretary. At the age of ten, she had been a member of the Youth Choir, singing in the alto line. She was a bundle of energy and enthusiasm whom the church recognized as a potential leader.

"There is no need to request an emergency board meeting," Hank dismissed the idea. Like Peach, he too had passed through all the clubs. His bias was drill. He loved the military. He was a natural Drill Instructor and disciplinarian. He was as strapping as Doug was lean; dark-skinned with a heavy bass voice. "We would be in and out of the trail very quickly. The expedition would take us less than four hours. It is only two miles. Not a real hike. Also, the possibility exists that we would have to postpone it if the board did not meet," he further explained. "Next scheduled board meeting is not due before three weeks."

"And Investiture is scheduled before that," Doug enjoined.

"You can request an emergency board," Peach persisted.

Lost in the Hills

"Me? Lady, you forgot I do not sit on the board. Ranger class, remember. The AY Leader represents the Master Guide Leader on the board."

"Well, ask the AY Leader to request an emergency board. The board can meet after service this Sunday or Wednesday and we can go next Sunday."

"People, the reality is that if we do not complete this expedition tomorrow we would not be ready for investiture. You will not get your Guide pin without the Wilderness Master. It is a critical component. We are in a very awkward position here," Doug drawled.

"It will take less than four or five hours," Hank continued. "All we need to do is spread the map, set the compass, track our trail and head in. It is a pretty simple trail."

"Pretty simple trail? Hmmm…" Despite her petite frame, Peach was not intimidated by Doug with his sharp tongue, and Hank with his heavy tone. "I don't have much hiking supplies at home," she mused aloud. "Matches, yes; rope, maybe; and I am due for new hiking shoes. And I won't be getting up early to prepare a meal to carry tomorrow, either."

Hank laughed. "You won't be needing all of that."

"The end result is a *master* honor on your sash," Doug grinned at her. "You could at least do without food or a new pair of shoes for that accomplishment, can't you?"

She made a face at them before persisting in her original line of argument. "I still don't like the idea of not informing the church board." Peach was a stickler for policy and procedure. She had the makings of an OCD personality that carried with it a penchant for plans constructed on information and mapped out in detail;

plans which followed policy and procedure to the letter.

"It is a quick, simple thing," the free-spirited Hank repeated. "We will tell them about it when we return."

"I don't like the sound of that," Peach stuck to her premise. "Murphy's law. *Whatever can go wrong, will go wrong. And when you least expect it too!*" She pulled nervously at her hair that was styled in a bob around her angular face. *She needed this expedition mapped out. They needed to take the names to the church board. This should be done the right way.*

"You are too pessimistic Peach," Doug teased. "We'd be out in a wink".

She sighed heavily. She was clearly outnumbered. Around her the rest of the club were silent.

After their quick planning session which went way beyond the ending of AY, Peach hurried home to return to the church compound to play basketball. She loved sporting activities. The youth hall facilitated a concrete yard where the youth of the church met on a Saturday night and during the week to engage in various sporting and social activities. Lately, basketball and football were the preferred Saturday night pastime. They played way beyond midnight; both young men and women of the church and community. She remained and played basketball with the guys late that night, uncaring that she had the hike scheduled for the following morning! The after effects were the lethargy and tiredness which she now felt, that had her longing to return to her bed when she should be bustling about, getting ready for their suddenly scheduled expedition.

Glancing at the clock adorning her room and realizing the lateness of the hour, she hastily shook herself out of her stupor, threw her slim, brown legs over the bed and dangled them,

Lost in the Hills

before reluctantly, but abruptly, getting out of the bed. That the end of the year was approaching, was evident from the chilly air wafting through the French windows that remained open in her bedroom, during the course of the night. On bare feet, she padded across to her wardrobe and tugged open the drawer, pulling out loose slacks and a light shirt. Yawning loudly, she threw them on the bed. Leaving her room, she rapped on her sister's bedroom door.

"Jade, wake up! You not hiking today or what?"

A groan was heard through the door. Peach pushed it in and dragged the blanket off her younger sister. "Girl, we late."

In an instant her sister was out of her bed. "What is the time?" she asked, even as she quickly neatened her bed.

"We have an hour to get to the walkover. No time for a proper breakfast. We would just grab *Crix* and cheese."

A smell permeated the house. They both inhaled, turned to each other and smiled. The aroma of daddy's fried eggs and mom's fried bakes wafted to their nostrils. No need to worry about breakfast. And they did not need to pack a lunch since the plan was to be out of the terrain by 12 noon anyway. *And she would finish her sleep then,* Peach smiled secretly. They dressed hurriedly, ensuring that they met the other members of the Club for 5am at the walkover on the Lady Young Road.

"Wait for me to pack you something," their father called out when they quickly dashed towards the door to exit the house.

"No need to; we'll be back around lunch time. That heavy fried bake and egg will keep us."

"You have enough water and supplies?" their mom echoed.

Lost in the Hills

"It is a short trail; not a regular hike; not at all grueling. We travelling light today."

With that, they raced out the gate and hustled to meet the hikers at the walkover. From there, a bus would take them to the starting point, west of the island; more specifically at the Macqueripe Bridge. At least, that is what she thought Doug had said. She was not very familiar with west Trinidad. Doug and a cadet would meet them later on, at the start of the hiking trail. In all, the group would comprise of fifteen: Hank, the Master Guide Leader, Doug, the Orienteering instructor, Hall, a cadet, members of the club comprising Eric, Jan, Judith, Dawn, Hazel, Cheryl, Michelle, Shelly, Wendy, Yvette, Jade, and Peach the Assistant Master Guide Leader. The imbalance was obvious — eleven women to just four men. But the women were sporty, assertive, brave and skilled, notwithstanding their varying sizes; Peach and Wendy the slimmest of them all, each barely boasting ninety pounds!

The sound of the surf west of the island was soothing; as they spread their maps, got their route cards and set their compasses. The damp smell of the earth was therapeutic as it fused into Peach's system. With a deep intake of breath, she looked around at the lush greenery of the rolling hills, the sparkling ocean decorated with triangular sails of the small boats; gently swaying effigies that made for a picturesque scene. They said a prayer and walked to the start of the trail, from where they were to break off into three groups to track a trail through to the designated location.

There were three groups. Group one consisted of the Master Guide Leader, Hank, along with Hazel, Michelle and Judith. Group two consisted of Jan, Yvette, Jade, Eric and Dawn. Group three was led by Peach, and Shelly, Wendy and Cheryl were her charges. A male was assigned to each group, except Peach's. From the start of the trail, and on to the satellite site, Peach complained:

Lost in the Hills

"Ours is the smallest group with the skinniest women and no male. That making sense?"

"You are the leader and you can handle your stories," Doug grinned.

"Am I hearing correctly?" she sighed. "We are all bony in this group. I am barely 90 pounds. Look at Wendy; she is probably 93 pounds. And Shelly and Cheryl are no more than 100 pounds. And on top of that, our group has the least members," she feistily rebutted. "Male or female we need brawn; whichever gender comes packaged with it."

"Girl, what you worrying about? Nothing would happen. Is a short trail. Plus, you could never lose with a map and a compass."

The sound of a pickup truck heading in their direction temporarily curtailed her complaining. The hikers enthusiastically waved their hands at the driver, who good-naturedly stopped. They scrambled into the tray, hitching a ride to Covigne Trail.

On arrival, Hank and Doug went ahead to check out the trail while the rest of the Master Guides in Training waited expectantly. Peach smiled smugly at the news they shared on their return, "The trail is already trampled so it makes no sense moving out in groups." Too many footpaths were present, and it was not as forested as they had hoped. "On another occasion, we would do the exercise in groups, in an unknown trail. For this expedition, however, we would proceed as one unit, but still fulfilling the requirements," Doug instructed.

Peach smiled, inwardly purposing that once in possession of her honor, absolutely no one was going to lose her up in any mountain with a map and a compass! As they set out, however, she did not find the trail difficult. Although bushy, it was not

Lost in the Hills

heavily forested. There were several footpaths as opposed to the one footpath the map presented. Hopefully, as they went further in, it would resemble the map a bit more. This was a critical component in the use of the compass and the determining of direction. The trail should echo the map; or vice versa.

They hiked slowly, chattered jovially, and laughed, giggled and clowned as they proceeded as one unit. The trail was muddy, but that was expected, given that it was November. In addition, the rainy season had been particularly active that year. Hurricane Kate was the latest in a total of nine hurricanes to hit that year, all attributed to la Nina which was blamed for several hurricanes and deaths the previous season, and which was expected to cause an intensification of weather patterns in the coming years. As usual, however, their tropical paradise had been spared storms and hurricanes, though they did occasionally experience ITCZs and tropical depressions that felled trees, caused landslips and flooded parts of the islands. It was expected that mud and bush would characterize the trail; that erosion would be a natural outcome after a dry spell that brought with it several bush fires, browning the hills, and leading to deforestation. With the rains would come soil erosion, culminating in massive landslips from the water-logged and loose earth. As good Master Guides, however, they had in their possession, three cutlasses, a coil of rope and a few bandages in case of injury. It was to be a half day affair anyway. *What other supplies would they need?* A fully-stocked First Aid kit they had overlooked and trivialized in their sudden and hasty planning of what they perceived as a short, simple hike.

Alas, fifteen minutes into the trail, they were called together and told that for the rest of the journey, they would be divided into two main groups after all. Peach's spirits sank. A sense of foreboding descended. She pursed her lips, thinking hard. *What if one of the groups took the wrong track or read the bearing incorrectly? What would happen then?*

Lost in the Hills

"I don't agree," she impetuously voiced her concern. "I don't have a good feeling about this. Let us remain as one unit Doug. The path does not even reflect the map."

But again, the confident pronouncement was thrown at her - *you could never lose with a map and a compass.* She wasn't so sure. This map was far different from the trail they were trekking. The group was split into two: Group one now consisted of Jan, Eric, Yvette, Jade, Wendy, Judith and Cheryl. Group two consisted of Hank, Michelle, Hazel, Dawn, Shelly and Peach.

The first group was sent off. Jade and Wendy lagged back to hike with Peach and Shelly. Hank, however, had learnt of their intentions so he hastened them off, but not before they had conspiratorially whispered to Peach and Shelly that they would hide further on in the terrain and wait for them. Doug also overheard their second plan and so, instead of waiting ten minutes for the first group to make headway, he commanded the second group to wait for fifteen minutes instead, before they proceeded. By then it was 10:30am. A driver was scheduled to meet the group at 12 noon when they were expected to exit the trail.

"Why did they split us up?" Shelly complained. "Look at the time. We won't make it out at 12, plus I have a function to attend later and I cannot be late."

"Hmm." Peach stubbornly folded her arms, pursed her lips and lapsed into silence. But her tempestuous, impulsive temperament did not allow her to stay quiet for long when irate, "I hate hiking slow and Doug knows it." An avid physical fitness freak, she could not bear hiking slowly. Whenever they hiked she was always up front with Jade.

"What wrong with you, you pessimists," Doug teased, hustling off to meet the first group. "You are a strong team. Wait fifteen

Lost in the Hills

minutes before proceeding," he reiterated his command.

"But we don't have much time," Shelly persisted. "It is already almost 11am and we have to meet Junior at 12noon by North Post Road."

"We will reach out in time," he called back as he hurried off.

Fifteen minutes later, they set out. As they swiftly progressed, Peach noted that the trail was becoming difficult. A path was no longer visible. Bushes and shrubs were all around. There were no landmarks. The sameness was unnerving. She hoped the compass was properly set. Based on their settings they were following the correct course.

Before long, they caught up with the first group which was proceeding slowly, given the uncertainty and the constant need to consult the map to ensure they were on the right path.

"Well, we are one unit after all," she wryly muttered to Doug. "At least we would be together should problems develop. Have you noticed that the trail does not resemble the map?" she reiterated. "Soil erosion, bush fires and man-made influences have altered the terrain."

"I noted that," he said soberly.

Cautiously they proceeded, with Doug and Hall in the lead, closely followed by Jade, Peach, Wendy, Shelly and Cheryl. Eric was in the middle section and Hank brought up the rear. The men felt it necessary to distribute themselves evenly among the women. Chivalry was still commonplace.

Mere moments after ascending a slippery incline, to their dismay, a fallen tree that was now a big log, was blocking their footpath.

Lost in the Hills

"Get the rope," Doug barked.

The hikers debated among themselves. "Which knot should we use? Clove hitch, overhand, simple loop?"

"Look just tie whatever could get us over quick yes." Shelly was anxious to get to her event later that evening.

Her outburst lightened the moment and quelled their anxiety. Loud laughter erupted.

"How you intend to get the rope around a log that size? I am sure there are snakes below that wet mossy log." Dawn said sardonically.

"Snakes!" Yvette screamed.

Peach laughed uproariously before pointing to a tree that stood on the incline just above the log. "Someone just needs to climb atop the log and pass the rope around that tree over there for us to haul ourselves over."

Hank took one end of the rope, deftly jumped up and over the log, found a sturdy limb and executed a slip knot. Peach tugged on it to ensure it jammed.

"You go first Peach," Doug commanded.

"So I am the guinea pig,' she rebutted in characteristic feisty fashion, even as she grabbed the rope, hauled herself up and over the log to the other side. In turn, each hiker followed suit. The opposite side was damp, forested and eerie. Hank and Hall nevertheless forged ahead, cutting foliage as they went through. Frustration descended when, having advanced for ten minutes the statement was made, "I think we are going the wrong way."

Lost in the Hills

Groans ascended. They trudged back through the dense foliage. In replacing the cutlass, Hall's palm inadvertently made contact with the sharp blade. Blood spilled from the serrated gash. That was a tragedy they neither needed nor anticipated.

"Peach!" Doug called.

"Jan, come!" Peach urgently called on the First Aid expert in the group. A gentle soul, she was the most senior member of the team who was on top of her First Aid game, given the fact that she had three very active sons.

"What bandage should she use?" Doug asked.

"He think we in club meeting," Wendy snickered.

Shelly giggled. "If I know we were getting a quiz I would have walked with my notes to revise."

"The figure of eight bandage is the best at this point." Jan said in her soft tone. "I will pad the wound before applying the bandage to hold it in place."

"Why?" Hank picked up where Doug left off.

"Good grief. What is all this interrogation about?" Dawn sighed.

But Jan was not fazed by their interrogation. "The injured area needs to be cushioned. It will also stop the blood and in this terrain we do not want contamination." She finished tying the bandage.

"Let's move on," Peach implored. "Time is ticking away. We have a maxi to meet, remember. At the rate we are going, we will not make it out before 12:30pm."

Lost in the Hills

Her comment resulted in crestfallen features from Shelly. Almost simultaneously with the realization, came the first sharp descent. Yvette gasped. Wendy gaped.

"Down there!" Everyone chorused as though on cue.

"Would you prefer to go up?" Doug sweetly teased.

There was no alternative. Bowline, two half hitches, double overhand knots. The practical uses of the sturdy hitches became real to the group of Master Guides in Training. They swung anxiously, but expertly, down the rope. Sickeningly aware of the time, the map and compass were hardly consulted.

Two young men approached the group. Everyone stilled as they observed their approach with suspicion. They were dressed in commando wear and large back packs were strapped to their bodies.

"They look like they walk out of a Brad Pitt, Sylvester Stallone or Arnold Schwarzenegger movie," Peach sardonically snickered.

"Yeah, right," Doug drawled, observing the duo intently.

The young men greeted the group of silently observing hikers.

"We are on a mission."

"What mission?" Doug stoically questioned.

"We had to spend the night here in the mountains, relying totally on the elements for food and water. It is part of our training. We completed it. We are now on our way out. Are you heading out or in?"

"Out."

Lost in the Hills

"What route?"

"We are following the map." Evasively.

"The map? This trail has changed a lot."

They were right about that. Doug nodded affirmation. Seeing his uncertainty, they offered, "We know of a shortcut. We can guide you out."

The driver was waiting. They were racing against time. They had utilized the map and compass for a major part of the expedition also. It was just the land slip that had thrown them off. They had covered more than the one mile required for the honor and the club members were pretty knowledgeable in the use of the devices.

The offer was accepted. Compasses were put away. It was

approaching 1pm; an hour behind the time they had planned on exiting. The log blocked the official trail. The shortcut seemed a viable option. Despite misgivings, they followed the *commando cadets.*

Chapter II - The Shortcut

The rain began to fall. Their clothes stuck to their bodies. Groans arose. No one had bothered to pack a change of clothes. They had expected to be out by noon.

"If we were out as scheduled, we would not be wet," Shelly lamented.

"If you had packed a proper hiking bag and worn proper hiking shoes, you would not have to complain," Hank rebutted.

"You said it would be a short, simple hike," Shelly refuted.

"Matters not. A hiker must always be prepared," Hank said firmly.

Lost in the Hills

"You told us we would be out by 12. Why should we pack lunch and a change of clothes?"

"Because a Master Guide must always be prepared for any eventuality." He was unmoving.

"You mean like Murphy's law? Like being lost? I told you I had a bad feeling about this from the beginning,"

"You and your *goat mouth*," Doug chastised.

Everyone went silent as they trekked uphill and downhill. After the third detour, Doug turned to the cadets, "You sure you know where you are going?"

A tent loomed ahead.

"Let us ask the farmer to show us the shortest and quickest way out," the cadets suggested to Doug.

"Why would they need to ask for directions if they claim to know a shortcut?" Peach asked suspiciously.

"I was thinking the same thing," Wendy whispered conspiratorially. "Why are we following them?" Worriedly.

"Because we desperate. And we have no choice now," Shelly said morosely. "We dispensed with the map and the compass so...um...where are we now?"

"We should have never listened to them," Jade grumbled. "We were good on our own. True the log set us off target and we were a little behind time, but we were doing well. Shortcut always get people in trouble."

"And there are no landmarks. Even if we were to return to map and compass, how would we get our bearing?" Peach sighed. "We are truly dependent on those two *Bollywood stars* now."

"You mean Hollywood?"

"Whatever. Same imitation."

"Didn't you see how they were playing commandos, bursting through the bushes and rolling on the ground? Good grief, they bring us up here to lose us?" Wendy's fine voice became even more high-pitched in her worry.

"They better just ensure I get home with enough time to shampoo and style my hair for my event later," Shelly asserted.

Peach laughed. "The way things looking, we spending the night here yes. Forget that event Shelly. At the rate we going, your date is with this hilly terrain tonight."

"Pessimist." The hikers turned on Peach as she laughed mischievously.

Their targeted time to be out of the mountains was now 1:30pm. While Doug, Hank, Hall and the cadets made their way to a small tent to enquire of the occupants about the shortest path out, the hikers exhausted the last of their minimal snacks.

"Hopefully the driver returns late," Dawn muttered.

"I doubt. Junior is always on time."

Doug returned shaking his head wryly, "There was no one in the tent."

The two cadets continued leading them out. Peach, Jade, Wendy, Cheryl and Shelly, who were always swift and in front, followed them. Doug and Hall led the middle group. Hank and

Lost in the Hills

Eric brought up the rear. Another incline dipped down ahead of them! Carefully, they made their way down the muddy, slippery embankment without use of the rope, crossed a few hills and jumped a few logs when the command, "Wait here!" was heard. But this time it was from Doug. He and Hall went up. The two cadets went down. The hikers waited uncertainly. Minutes later the two cadets returned urgently. Doug and Hall were not in sight.

"Hurry." they whispered. "We have to get away from here quick."

"Why?" Peach questioned in bewilderment.

"This is a gold mine you know," the cadet continued, urgently. "This is dangerous territory."

"What do you mean by *gold mine*?" Peach sought clarification.

In the absence of Doug and Hank, she was the next leader in line. *Just what were they talking about?*

"It's a marijuana patch," Michelle explained.

Peach clutched her chest. "People usually got shot going through those plantations," she blurted.

Oh gosh, what would happen to them? What if the owner came back? Her heart pounded frantically. *What had they gotten themselves into?*

"Hank said wait here so I'm not going anywhere." Hazel said stubbornly.

Peach looked around anxiously, wondering what to do. *To go or not to go?*

Lost in the Hills

"Hurry!" The cadet said a little louder. "Let's get out of here fast!"

The urgency in his voice determined her response. *Why wait when there was a way out; Mattered not if they went or waited, they could be shot, couldn't they? Either way they were in danger.*

"Let's go," she commanded. Hank and Doug would catch up with us. It is our only way out. We can't go up to get out."

"I waiting for Doug and Hank," Hazel stubbornly asserted.

"Well meet us when they return. Show them the path we took."

Wendy, Shelly, Jade, Cheryl and Peach raced along behind the cadets, down through the plantation, while Hazel remained behind, blocking the others from following since she was next in line. They were halfway down the track when they heard Hazel shouting, "Hank said to come back up. He is calling us!"

"Tell them to meet us down here!" Peach shouted back at her.

"What he want us to come up for. That making any sense? Up doesn't lead out." Wendy's limited patience was running thin.

Frustrated and angry Peach hissed, "This is real nonsense!"

The two cadets went their way. Hazel and the other hikers left to follow Hank who had received instructions from Doug and Hall. The five hikers stood undecided in the middle of the *plantation*, pondering their next move.

"Let's follow the cadets," Wendy urgently instructed.

"But the others not coming. Look they leaving," the normally quiet Cheryl interjected.

Lost in the Hills

"We have to hike as one group," Peach logically stated. "We cannot split up like this. As much as I want to follow them, we have to go back up."

By then the cadets had disappeared and the rest of the group were moving away from sight.

"Hurry. We have to go back up," Peach urgently instructed. "If you hear gunshots, roll like *Hunter* and the other detectives do on television, to avoid being shot," Although she said it jokingly to lighten the moment, her heart was thumping. Trap guns and other such devices were normally planted in fields like the one in which they were running through. *Oh gosh, they could be shot!* As she moved hastily through the dense foliage bearing trees way above her height, her eyes scanned the bushes for a line, a twine, any evidence of a trap. Her toes twitched, feet alert for the feel of any object. Her chest constricted. What if she stepped on an object fastened to a rifle located anywhere near her? Detonation could be triggered by one incorrect step! Her heart thudded. *"Please God, don't let me be shot,"* she internalized a prayer.

Hazel looked smugly down on them as they scrambled up to the waiting hikers.

"I told you to wait," she blurted.

"Whatever," Shelly disdainfully retorted.

"And they would get out while we spend the night in these hills," Wendy angrily rebutted." We should have followed them if we wanted to make it out on time."

"If we wanted to make it out at all," the normally silent Cheryl said pensively.

Chapter III – Things Go Wrong!

Caught up in no man's land,

Don't know where to stand...

Yvette's morose melody matched their glum faces. The mood darkened further when Doug returned with a nasty gash which ran from his index finger to his palm. Blood oozed. It looked more serious than Hall's had been. Jan dipped into the first aid kit and immediately applied pressure on the wound with a clean cloth, in an attempt to stop the bleeding. Precious water, warm from the heat of the day, and limited in supply, was poured on the wound to clean it. Because of the location of the wound, two sterile bandages were used to protect it. Peach sighed worriedly. *The two most experienced persons were injured,*

Lost in the Hills

both in their hands and both by cutlasses! And their supply of limited bandages was running terribly low. What next?

Next was an uphill climb.

"But it's down we want to go." Wendy grumbled. As time ticked by, her patience thinned further.

"Down holds danger," Doug firmly stated. His finger was injured, not his mouth. His commanding tone was as strong as ever.

With a lot of sliding and screaming the hikers went up, and up, and up. Locating a landmark was their major priority. They were now, once more, in need of the map and the compass. The *Shortcut* had thrown them off their course. On a relatively flat slope, they spread their once-discarded maps and pulled out their compasses, trying re-orient themselves. They compared the physical features around them with the map, to help them discover their location. To their dismay, while the map suggested one footpath, around them there were several, given the use of the terrain by various *members of the public*. Apart from trees, rivers and one footpath, there were no other landmarks from which they could have located their bearing. In essence, the map and compass were useless, unless they located their correct position. It was now 3pm. They continued climbing. An elevation no doubt would provide a good vantage point from which to seek out a landmark and orientate themselves; at least that is what they hoped going up, not down, would yield – the only way down was through the *plantation* anyway.

Peach tried keeping their spirits high by singing. Michelle, a jovial personality, joined her and they sang *"We are going to make it."* They climbed on their knees, occasionally using vines for support as they ascended higher and higher. It was essential that a bearing was located: the sea, a tower, anything from which their location could be ascertained and a course mapped out.

At the top of an incline, they had their first conference session. With occasional electrifying and dizzying glances downward, they listened in trepidation as Doug spoke.

"People, I don't have to tell you what we all know; that right now our compass is of no use and we are just going around in circles, feeling our way out. We are totally dependent on the help of God, through prayer, to make it out of here."

"All because of a *shortcut*," Jade sighed.

They formed a circle, held hands, sang *"Sweet Hour of Prayer"* and prayed. After the prayer, Doug shocked the group by announcing, "People, we are continuing up!"

"Again!" Aghast.

"There?"

"How?"

"Why?"

Above them was a steep slope, and being already high up they knew that if any of them were to fall there was no hope of survival. In fact, if you fell, as the local parlance went, *"yuh dead for sure."* Pointed pine trees lay like a prickly bed far, far below. In fact, truth be known, up was the only direction they could have taken, since down was a very long way. Hopefully, they would see one of the islands off Trinidad and this would help them locate their position. A few of the hikers cried. The majority were worried. The tension was eased when Jade suddenly exclaimed, "What are you all frightened for? We will

Lost in the Hills

all reach home in time for *Three's Company* at least. Watch and see."

Three's Company was Sunday evening's prime time comedy on *TTT*, the local television station. *Solid Gold* usually followed on the heels of *Three's Company* – or was it the other way around? Everyone started laughing. A bowline was tied. They couldn't risk slippage or jams. A slip knot was too unpredictable, given the gravity of the situation. They held on to the rope, and swung up, not looking down, where the thorny, deadly bed of pines was the only view. When they finally made it to the top and were on solid footing, they turned left, expecting to see the sea shimmering in the sparkling sun. Instead, they encountered the vast expanse of the blue sky, resplendent in all its glory, stretching for miles, reflecting the color of the invisible ocean that seemed to be hiding from them, leaving them at the mercy of the mountains that now entrapped them.

"The shadow tip method," someone intoned

"And even if we locate North, what next?" Peach sighed. "We don't just want to know where North is, we need to find a trail to get us out. We need a landmark so the map can be of use."

"This map is useless. We just need to move and cut a trail out," Hank stated in a matter-of-fact tone. "We can't go through the people *plantation,* so we have to create an alternative route out. That's just about the size of it."

So they began their descent on the opposite side of the mountain, cutting their way through, time ticking away too quickly for their liking. They thirsted for the sight of a house, a road, just one iota of civilization. At 5:15pm they came upon a clearing. Someone started singing *Free at Last,* but when they looked around, instead of being free, they found themselves ensnared by mountains and dense foliage. Panic was evident on all the faces. The atmosphere was dismal. Dusk was descending quickly in the mountains that Sunday in November, close to the end of the year.

They quickened their pace as they headed downhill, following what appeared to be the sound of a river. The river, they felt, must lead somewhere. It did. Down over a precipice into a waterfall. The other side led to a dead end. It was too late to continue cutting a path. Premature darkness descended. They retraced their steps to the clearing. Jade lost feeling in both her legs as the urgent cry was heard, "Hurry, it's getting dark fast."

As they grouped on the clearing, reality hit them like a whip. They would not make it home that night. Their hastily planned half day expedition had turned into an unplanned overnight wilderness camp. Nine of them sat on a cold, wet log; the others stood around. Everyone was silent. It was 6pm and already completely dark in the forested hills. They were not home; nor would they get home that night; nor was it the era of cell phones, so they couldn't call for help. They had nothing to eat or drink; no warm clothes. A cold wet log would be their bed; if they ever slept. There would be no school or work or regular Monday morning activities the following day. *What if rain were to fall? And what of their parents and loved ones?*

Wordlessly, Peach regretfully ruminated. The sight of her bed flashed before her. She had planned to return to it early and sleep. She should be in it now; not lost and stranded in hilly terrain, stuck in wet clothes and shoes with no lunch and no shelter. Then it suddenly struck her... *What of the church board? Oh goodness! By now parents would be frantically calling around! So much for getting in and out quickly. The adage was correct!* "Be sure your sins would find you out!"

"We are going to get it when we return. You know that right Hank? We did not tell the board of this and now the untenable has happened. *Murphy's law* has kicked in, just as I sensed."

"You have real *goat mouth* yes Peach." Hank shook his head wryly.

"I just sensed this would happen. I just sensed it," Peach repeated dazedly.

In the silence of the mountains, they drank in faint sounds of civilization that intermittently floated up to them based on the direction of the wind. Occasionally, they indistinctly heard the distant sounds of dogs barking, cars moving, music playing.

"Anyone have anything to eat at all?" Dawn asked.

"My Sunday lunch. At home," Peach groaned.

"I have a half bottle of juice," Cheryl volunteered.

"Well we were supposed to be out at 12," Wendy whined. "We were told we could walk light, ent Hank?"

"Hikers must always be prepared. Hike as though it is an all-day event. Always be prepared for an emergency," Hall said quietly. "Where are your bags? And those who have bags, where are your ropes, your change of clothes, your water. Look at your shoes, all light and water-soaked. Your toes are wet. So are your clothes. Where are your coats? Isn't it rainy season? Where are your hiking shoes?"

No one responded. He was correct. They had treated the hike lightly and broken all the rules.

"Are there wild animals up here?" Judith asked, craftily trying to escape the chastisement.

Yvette gasped and clutched her stomach. "Oh gosh. Don't say

that girl."

"Maybe the giant Macajuel snake," Hall deliberately drawled. "It big like a log. I heard a story once of some hikers that sat on a log and were swallowed when they fell asleep, since it turned out the log was a sleeping snake. That is why when persons overeat, they say they feel like a Macajuel. That snake eats its belly full and sleeps looking like a log, only to awaken to eat again. It is a constrictor." Hall was brutal. All who were sitting on the log jumped off. He glanced across at Peach who was smothering a laugh, and grinned.

"You lying man Hall," Wendy accused even though she was the first to jump off the log.

"We need to start a fire," Jan said in a matter-of-fact tone. "That will scare away the wild animals. I think up here have tiger cats and wild monkeys."

Yvette screamed out again.

"I have a box of matches in my bag," Hank said jovially, pulling out a box. "I am always prepared for any eventuality. I packed properly. Didn't you all learn anything from your leader?"

"People, you should know how to accumulate dry tinder and kindling despite wet conditions. Gather material, let us start a fire," Doug instructed.

"A fire to last all night," Peach interjected. "Not the little firewood you generate when we go on our half day, outdoor skills and cooking expeditions. This fire is for warmth, scaring away animals and possibly an SOS."

"SOS Peach?" Hank laughed.

"Hopefully. You never know," Peach sheepishly rebutted.

Lost in the Hills

"Wish this were a hoax like the last expedition," Jade mumbled.

"Well, you cried wolf. It came. Take it." Hank laughed referring a prior expedition when a young pathfinder had faked a broken leg and the prank had gone much further than she had bargained for.

"Try not to pick up snakes when you are collecting the firewood people," Peach wickedly teased when the hikers pushed aside the surrounding bush and shrubs seeking dry kindling, tinder and firewood. She giggled at the gasps from Yvette and a few frightened others who hastily grabbed what they could and deposited it in front of the log for Peach, Hall, Hank and Doug to organize. Hank struck the first match. It flickered and went out. He struck another one. The same thing happened. "People I only have one more match," he confessed.

"Like you buy your *Friend* pin. We better fire you yes," Shelly exclaimed.

"Ooh, I love it! A perfect pun!" Peach laughed and clapped.

The literary device was lost on Shelly who, irate for having missed her event carded for that night, turned on Hank, "Oh you always prepared and all you have is three matches in a box."

"Three plumes literally and symbolically," Peach tried keeping the atmosphere light by deliberately joking and jesting, prolonging the pun.

"*Fire me?* You better pray." Hank laughed. "Because if this one doesn't light, we have nothing to scare away the tiger cats, wild monkeys and snakes that this terrain is known for. The Coral is venomous, the Macajuel will swallow you and the Tigre will run you down, along with the tiger cat."

Lost in the Hills

Yvette whimpered.

"Boy don't make serious joke like that nuh," Dawn chastised.

"Somebody else strike that match please," Yvette begged.

Hank laughed wickedly.

"Let's worship," Doug said quietly.

The atmosphere stilled. They sang. They prayed in groups of two. Then they circled the well positioned kindling, tinder and firewood blocking out the chilly night air. Hank firmly struck the last match. The tinder caught. The kindling flared. The firewood crackled. The log coaled. The coals were fanned. A flame flickered and flared. A sigh of relief escaped the group of fifteen. Shoes came off to be placed around the camp fire to dry.

"I remember a hiker who was on an expedition like we are now. He took his shoes off to place by the fire to dry. When he put them back on the following morning he felt a sharp sting. A scorpion had crawled in. Needless to say he lost his big toe." Hall was on a roll with his anecdotes.

Wet shoes were replaced on cold toes. Hank, however, was not fazed by his legend, or anecdote or whatever it was. He left his boots by the fire. "All you have to do is knock the shoes before putting them back on people. What's the fuss?" He flippantly asserted.

"Let's stargaze," Peach suggested. "Look at that literal blanket of stars. Ooh! I have never seen it this pretty! I cannot even locate Orion."

Heads turned upward. Oohs and aahs were heard when the hikers encountered the beauty of the sky. A million stars twinkled

Lost in the Hills

down on them.

"You can even see the Milky Way. We don't get see it with the interference of man-made lights. We really need the bright stars in these constellations to point them out here boy. Let's locate Sirius first. The brightest star." Peach was excited at the opportunity for a real stargazing session. It reminded her of her childhood days, sitting in the yard with her siblings and dad, he with his star chart, pointing out *Orion*, and *Andromeda* and *Cassiopeia* (the Lady in the Chair) and other constellations.

"There it is!"

"From Sirius, locate the other stars in the winter triangle. Then we can map the constellations. If only we had a bright torchlight to point them out. This is really a good, practical stargazing exercise here. It is beautiful," Peach breathed.

"There is Betelgeuse. Look for the orange-red star," Hank instructed.

"And Procyon," Yvette's fear of wild animals and creepy-crawlies momentarily abated, caught up as she was in the star-gazing exercise. "Ooh there is Orion. You have to identify all the bright stars to find him boy. Bellatrix, Betelgeuse, Riguel and Saiph. Without those bright stars, Orion would be lost in this darkness. And there is Big Dog!"

"Isn't it amazing," Peach gushed. "When we are in the city all we see is the barest outline of the constellations. Here we can even make out the other parts of the dog and the belt. It is as though you can lie on the blanket of stars. I can now understand that song by *The Pointer Sisters*," she giggled.

"What song?" Doug looked at her suspiciously.

Lost in the Hills

Peach instantly dreamily crooned:

> ... On shadowed ground, with no one around
> And a blanket of stars in our eyes
> We are drifting free, like two lost leaves
> On the crazy wind of the night...

"Girl, you in a real mess yes," Doug shook his head. "Who you drifting free with?"

"Not a soul," Peach drawled sardonically. "I just loving the symbolism. Nothing else! I good by myself. I don't need nobody to drift with."

"You so cynical eh girl," Doug chastised.

"He who expects little is never disappointed. I good as I am."

"Until you get ketch."

"Yeah, right. Never! Those ideal qualities introduced to us in the session on *choosing a life partner* don't exist in just one person. We have come a long way since Eden."

"What ideals?" Doug asked, bemused.

"Loves the Lord, chaste, faithful, honest, industrious, good communicator, sense of humor, understanding, family person, hygienic, sensitive, spiritual, conflict resolution skills, just to name a few."

"A few! You expect to get all the ideals in one person Peach?" Hank drawled.

"Nope," Cockily. "That is why I good just as I am – Single and free."

Lost in the Hills

The sound of a helicopter was heard.

"Maybe they're looking for us." Judith said hopefully, reminding them of their hopeless situation.

"Don't bet on it. A Missing Persons report can be lodged only after 48 hours. No one but our parents know that we are up here."

"Let's shout for help to get their attention," Wendy suggested.

Without waiting for consent to her suggestion she shouted, "Help!!!!!"

Peach laughed.

She turned to the others standing around looking at her. "That must be them looking for us. Come on people, let us shout to get their attention. Help!!!!"

A few persons joined her. Peach doubled over in laughter as they shouted, some joining in just for the fun of it and laughing along with Peach.

Wendy stopped shouting only when the sound of the helicopter faded. "Yes, go ahead and laugh," she chastised. "I tell you they were looking for us."

"Yeah, right; like I said 48 hours. If they do not see us by tomorrow, then they may start looking. We on our own tonight. This log is our bed."

"You real know how to dash people hopes yes," Hazel muttered.

"I smelling something burning." Hank twisted his nose. "It

Lost in the Hills

smelling like.... like...rubber? Oh gosh....my boots!"

The stress was once again alleviated as everyone burst out laughing. As the fire blazed, the heat had started melting his boots. He smelt it just in the nick of time. Although slightly burnt they were still wearable.

"People I think I calling it a night," Peach said sleepily. Having played basketball until late, then awakening early for their trek, she was very tired. Notwithstanding the absence of a bed, her eyes drooped.

"Calling it a night? You not serious," Doug looked at her incredulously, and burst out in raucous laughter.

"Boy, I sleepy," she murmured, bending her head on the shoulder of Hank who was now sitting next to her on the log. Jade was sitting next to Peach. She placed her head on Peach's shoulder. Peach fell asleep in quick time. Jade fell asleep soon afterwards. Others also followed suit and eventually they fell asleep on each other's shoulder. When necks and shoulders became stiff they switched to laps. That was the sleeping pattern throughout the night.

.

A rustling sound. Peach stirred. It was coming from the grass ringing them. Her heart thumped erratically in her chest. *Tiger cats?* Jade was racing towards her from the direction of the bushes wide-eyed in fear.

"I saw a man, in white, standing staring at us."

"What?" Peach asked groggily, waking up cramped to find that her head was now resting on Hazel's shoulder to her left. During the night persons got up and switched positions as Peach

Lost in the Hills

slept continuously.

Jade's eyes were wide. "A man in white was just standing, staring at us. Over there!" She pointed to a particularly dark area, in the direction of a region they had not explored. Something...someone... in white...over there!" Verbs were left out in her haste to communicate the cause of her fright.

"In white?" Peach echoed dazedly.

Jade squeezed her way in between Peach and Hazel. Everyone was now silent.

Meanwhile, down the mountains, across the nation, unknown to them, they were the headline news on Television and radio; News that was repeated all through the night and into the next day. **Lost in the Hills ... young hikers missing!**

Chapter IV – The Dawn of A New Day

At 5am they were up. Songs of worship permeated the hills, notwithstanding their situation. Each person gave their opinion on the experience. Pensively, they acknowledged it was a faith-strengthening exercise. Scriptural promises were shared. Prayerfully, they sought God's leading in finding their way out of the labyrinth, trapped as they were, high up, between several mountains in the northern range. Hall, who was not a member of their faith, indicated his admiration of their spirit and togetherness. He compared them to other groups who, under similar conditions, reacted far differently. Notwithstanding the circumstances, he was enjoying the experience with them.

After worship they pooled whatever little money they had, since they presumed the driver had left.

Lost in the Hills

"No taxi would pick us up in this condition anyway," Peach said wryly. "Look at our muddy, disheveled, unkempt appearance. We may as well prepare to hike straight to our homes. And good grief our breaths smell. Not even toothpaste."

"I have mints," Cheryl volunteered.

Two dinner mints were divided between the fifteen hikers.

"I have a comb and a mirror. A good hiker is always prepared, ent Hank?" Peach laughed mischievously and made a face at her disheveled reflection in the mirror. *Gosh, she looked bad.*

"What that good for?" He rebutted looking at her aghast. "You too vain. A mirror on a hike!"

"We could at least neaten up ourselves before facing the public." Perkily.

"You too much trouble for me yes." In resignation.

"Well people, this morning the only way we are going is down; down must lead somewhere."

"And hopefully, we'd be out before 9am." Jan muttered.

"And we not telling anyone we were lost. We will just say we took a wrong turn. The conference must never know of this; only our relatives and local church members." Peach affirmed.

"But we were not lost," Jan intoned. "We were going good until we decided to follow those cadets."

"Shortcuts always bring trouble," Jade repeated.

Everyone heartily agreed.

Lost in the Hills

"Could you imagine if the conference Youth Director ever found out about this? He would make us a public spectacle." Peach widened her eyes and clutched her heart dramatically.

"Let's move!" Doug was rearing to go.

As they turned from the plateau to make their descent down the track, fresh footprints were visible on the muddy track! The footprints weren't their own! They had not taken that path before!

"Someone was here during the night," she heard Doug mention to Hall and Hank.

"The owner of the plantation, maybe," Hall intoned.

Peach turned to Jade. *Was it possible that Jade had witnessed the presence of an angel watching over them; protecting them from danger?*

"Let's hasten out of here folks." Doug's tone was soft and urgent. The bush did not only have ears, it appeared to have feet as well.

They had made good headway before the sun settled in the sky to ferociously blaze down, as was its daily habit, when not held in check by rain. In the distance, something silver shimmered; the galvanized roof of a dwelling; *a signal of civilization!*

"That's probably where the sounds came from last night," Peach stated.

"If that is the case, then we should be out of here before midday," Doug mused.

"Don't set no time again nuh," Wendy, having been bitten was now twenty times shy. "I not trusting anything you and Hank say again."

Hank laughed uproariously.

They continued their descent. The farther down they went, the farther down they had to go. They came to a river. Cheryl bent to drink.

"Nope." She looked quizzically at Doug who had instantly restrained her.

"Purification strategy. Where is it flowing from? Check for stagnancy."

"All of that? We thirsty. It looking clean." Wendy retorted.

"We have to identify a proper water source. You covered that in the Friend Class."

"I remember once we were hiking," Peach started giggling immediately as Hall began one of his many anecdotes in his usual drawl. He looked at her, smothered a laugh, and continued, "Someone saw water trickling down from a rock. The water was crystal clear. He drank. Someone looked up. His eyes made four with a man. The man was urinating in the water."

"Oh gosh man Hall!" Hazel chastised.

"My thirst gone," Cheryl morosely muttered. "I don't think I will be thirsty until I get home."

Uncontrollable laughter almost obliterated an unexpected call that echoed around the mountain, causing them to stop in their tracks.

Lost in the Hills

"Hello!!!!!!!"

In one unplanned accord they all responded "Hello!!!!!!!!!!!!!!!!" It was now 8:05am. They had been hiking downhill for two hours nonstop!

"How many of you?" The voice came again

"Fifteen!" Doug responded.

"Stay where you are." The voice faded.

Anxiously, they waited. *Who was/were the person/s that had come to lead them out of the mountains?*

"Where are you?"

"Follow the river!" Hank shouted. "We are on the left of the river."

Fifteen minutes later the voice was heard, but fainter.

"Are you Adventists...? Stay where you are...We'll be there soon..."

When soon turned to twenty minutes, they began to grow impatient.

"Who do you think they are?" Peach enquired of Doug. "How did they know we were up here?"

"Are you from the army?" Doug shouted.

No response.

"How many of you?" He shouted again.

Lost in the Hills

No response.

"Who are you?" He shouted desperately.

They were growing impatient and angry. "Like they don't even know where they are. They must be lost too." Peach laughed.

"We are the army..." Came the faint response.

When another five minutes passed with still no sign of anyone and the sound of the voices grew fainter and fainter instead of nearer and nearer, they reasoned among themselves, "It's those two *commando-playing-cadets*. If it was in fact the army they would have found us a long time ago," Hank sardonically declared.

"Let's continue down," Doug commanded after they had waited for thirty minutes.

"No, let's wait," Wendy argued. "Suppose it is really the army."

"Army?" Dawn sneered. "It is those two crazy cadets. They like to pretend that they're soldiers. I agree with Hank; if they were really soldiers, they would have found us a long time ago!"

"And neither soldiers nor police officers would come looking for us before 48 hours had elapsed anyway. We have been missing for *only* one night." Peach insisted.

Yet, for Wendy's sake, they waited.

"Stay where you are." The voice came faintly from way down in the valley below.

Sighing and sucking their teeth, they waited restlessly in the bushy, muddy terrain high up in the mountains. By then, forty-five minutes had been wasted just standing waiting, since the first call. At 9am, one hour later, everyone, including Wendy, was ready to move on.

"If it's the army they'll find us." They impatiently reasoned.

They continued down, bursting out in laughter a few minutes later when they heard the shout again. Hours later, still heading downhill, after crossing a river, they came upon a precipice. Peach groaned. She couldn't believe that after they had come so far down, there was still such a long way to go. Looking up she encountered endless hills and trees; looking down she encountered the top of trees and dense bushes. When she looked around she saw yet more trees and density, and looking across the precipice, she saw houses. It was almost 2pm. *How in the name of possibility were they going to get to those houses?*

Depression settled over her like a cloud. For the first time, her gaiety subsided. With a heavy sigh, she turned to Doug, "This is not good. We not making it out of here today."

It was the sound of her voice and the slump in her stance, more than her actual words, that had him instantly responding, "Peach, not you. You can't give up now. You have engendered energy throughout the experience, despite the situation. I am counting on you to keep the energy level of the others up. If you break, the positivity dies and right now we need positivity...I need positivity."

Breathing a prayer, she looked at the big black ants spilling out of the dense bushes that Hank was cutting through. "*Lord, get us out of this,*" she silently begged. She turned to look at the hikers.

"Ok," she smiled. "We going to make it, right, Michelle?"

Lost in the Hills

Michelle started singing again at the top of her voice, "*We are going to make it, We are going to make it.*" She didn't care who sang along with her. She sang loudly enough for all of them. It distracted them as they commented on her dry, out-of-tune voice.

"Thanks," Doug whispered to Peach.

She nodded.

"We will get out today, before dark. I promise you that."

"Don't make any promises," she cheekily rebutted.

"Can you see the house!"

"They still around?" Hazel laughed.

"That voice sounding familiar," Judith exclaimed.

"Yes!" Hank shouted.

"We are by the house. Where are you?"

"That's Leroy's voice." Doug and Peach shouted simultaneously. Leroy was the former Master Guide Leader and one of the current youth leaders. He was the brother of Peach and Jade, and the husband of Yvette.

"Is everyone okay?"

"Yes!" They shouted excitedly in chorus, believing the voices to belong to Leroy and other members of the district council. The Leader Don, the current AY Leader of the church, Michael, and maybe other youth leaders of the district had, no doubt, been informed by parents, and being former uniform members themselves, had come searching for them.

Lost in the Hills

"Hear them voices man. Hear them voices." Laughter was heard in the responses.

"So much for keeping this a secret," Peach muttered. "Now the entire district knows. For sure, they would tell the Youth Director. The untenable would be if he is there with them."

Doug laughed. "I doubt that very much.

Hank returned to the river with Peach and a few others to give directions while the rest of the hikers waited, since some were coming up the river and some up the precipice. *How?* They didn't know, but the thought of familiar faces and more help getting out, buoyed their spirits up.

To their amazement, instead of familiar faces from the youth district, two strange men decked in soldier's garb came up alongside the river. Peach froze in shocked bewilderment.

"Did the two cadets tell you that we were up here?" She questioned.

"Which two cadets?" They frowned. "We were called out of base this morning to come and get you all."

'Called out of base?" She asked confused. "Who called you out? I don't understand."

The light-skinned soldier laughed. "Since last evening, you all were reported missing, so we set out very early this morning."

"Last evening?" Peach echoed stupefied. "Reported missing? By whom?"

"You are all over the news – Television, Radio and Newspapers. In fact, the press is here waiting patiently for us to bring you out."

Lost in the Hills

Peach sagged. "Reporters? Here? They are down there waiting for us?"

"Yup," the soldier laughed. "From 7pm you were on the news every hour. Even a helicopter was out last night combing this area."

She stared at them, her mouth agape. *Wendy had been correct in her assertion the previous night!* "Even though 48 hours have not passed?"

"48 hours? From the minute you were reported missing we were put on alert. This is rough terrain. This is training ground for us. We also do target practice here. You all must have used rope to get to this side because this is pretty rugged terrain."

She froze before saying in a tremulous voice, "Okay. So the two of you are going to lead us out of here?"

"There are others with us," he said.

"More soldiers?"

"Combing the hills looking for you all...yes."

"So the entire country knows we are missing?" Bemused.

"The entire country." Amused

Peach groaned before questioning, "So what is the plan? How we getting out of here? It is already 3pm. We have been hiking down all day and there is still a long way down to go. How did you get up? Is there another trail we didn't see or the map did not identify?"

"Down there." The other soldier said in amusement. "With rope." He was very patient in the face of all her questions which were tumbling out even before answers were provided to the previous ones.

"There!" she pointed incredulously at the smooth rocks jutting out of the mountain.

"Yes." He said laughing. "Unless you want to go back up, and I'm sure you don't. All you have to do is grip the rope tightly and don't look down. We are going down, that's for sure."

"Tarzan personified," She gushed. Heart racing at the thought of the dizzying journey down, she followed the soldiers back to the precipice to meet the others. Jan, *the medical practitioner,* was bandaging the hand of one of the soldiers who had received a cut while coming up the stony incline.

"You all look as though you are enjoying yourselves." The soldiers laughed at their muddy, disheveled condition. "But you all look as fresh as ever."

"Yeah, right." Wendy snickered. "Mamaguy us."

"No, seriously. We expected to find a cowering, dejected probably injured crew of young people, especially given the nature of this terrain."

"So how are we getting out?" Wendy repeated the question Peach had asked.

"Down there." Calmly

Wendy's eyes widened. Yvette clutched her stomach. Jade groaned.

Chapter V – The Journey Down

Everyone stood silently atop the steep slope waiting for the signal to start moving as the rope was fastened. Instructions were provided. They were simple. "Hold on to the rope. Keep looking up. Don't look down."

The soldiers were strategically positioned all the way down the steep slope, holding on the rope like posts, assisting the hikers as they cautiously made their way down jagged, slippery rocks jutting out of the mountains. The sound of a helicopter was heard overhead. The national helicopter services was circling. They made the journey in three phases. It was on the third and final leg, which involved navigating their way down a very steep slope to the river, that they saw them patiently waiting across on the other side - family members, local and district youth leaders,

Lost in the Hills

and well-wishers, clapping, cheering them on and laughing at their condition. They rushed over to the hikers and one by one, enthusiastically embraced them. The media, who had also been quietly waiting, captured their images as they exited, seeking comments as they approached, just as the soldiers had indicated they would.

After the hugs and exuberant response, Doug went to the hospital to seek medical attention for his injured finger while the rest of the hikers made a mandatory trip, as instructed by the soldiers, to the police station. There, they were gently reprimanded.

"You should have registered before heading in. You know that...."

They had known, but had broken all the rules in their haste to be invested; and the shortcut had blown their cover.

"Soldiers take 24 hours to cover that terrain. It is rough. Had you retraced your steps you could have been shot, since that trail is used for target practice. You should have informed the nearest police station of your expedition," the stern officer repeated.

The hikers stood quietly, accepting the well-deserved reprimand. Peach's eyes fell on the clock over the counter - 3:30pm. *A half-day expedition had rolled into two days!*

"But we are glad you are ok," his face softened. "We are glad we found you alive and unharmed."

Impulsive Peach had a question of her own. She couldn't resist it. "Is it true that those mountains are the habitat of wild monkeys, tiger cats and macajuels?"

"Yes. That is true."

Lost in the Hills

Yvette gasped.

"Did you see any?" He cocked his head intently at them.

Everyone shook their heads.

"Well, you are fortunate. Your God must have been with you."

"It *WAS* an angel you saw," Peach breathed softly to Jade. "Truly, the eyes of the Lord are on the righteous and His ear is open to their cry".

Epilogue

When she was finally able to crawl into her beckoning bed later that night, Peach rolled over into her pillow. "We have some making up to do," she whispered, even as she stretched languidly out in the bed. A smile curved her lips as she drifted into slumber. *Home Sweet Home.* She drew her teddy bear to her chest and floated on a cloud of memories; her fluffy blanket – not a blanket of stars – covered her. School or no school, she would get out of that bed only when her body felt inclined to do so and the bed released her. And she would have her *Sunday Lunch* that her parents saved for her and Jade, whatever time she awoke during the following day.

Petra Pierre - Robertson

"Oh gosh darling!" Leroy hugs his wife Yvette playfully while Judith, last in line bends her head on seeing the camera. And Dawn, she smiles as usual while Cheryl, (in front) continues out.

"Thank God we're out!" Michelle, eyes closed, seems to be praying, while Jocelyn, second from right seems to be saying, "Are we really out Lord?!"

Seated from left are Wendy, Shelly, Michelle, Jocelyn and Petra. Oh, and those two eyes, directly in front belong to Jan McLean.

Lost in the Hills

Henry grins happily as Leroy welcomes him back; but you should have seen him in the mountains!

Petra Pierre - Robertson

What a magnificent view, you must think...Actually that's where we came out from.

Lost in the Hills

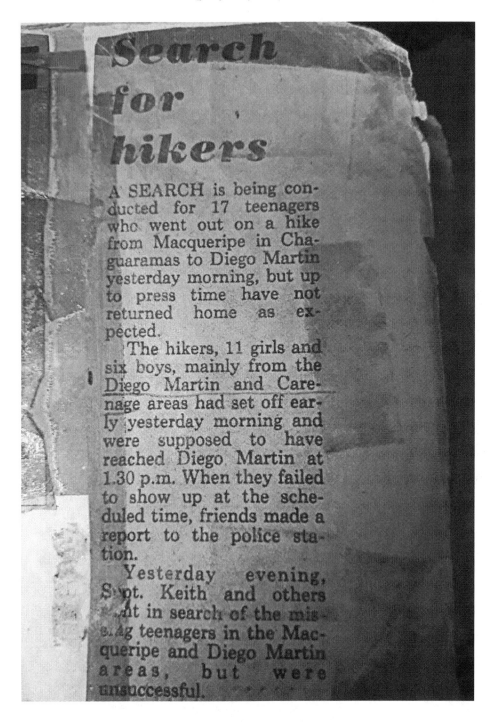

Search for hikers

A SEARCH is being conducted for 17 teenagers who went out on a hike from Macqueripe in Chaguaramas to Diego Martin yesterday morning, but up to press time have not returned home as expected.

The hikers, 11 girls and six boys, mainly from the Diego Martin and Carenage areas had set off early yesterday morning and were supposed to have reached Diego Martin at 1.30 p.m. When they failed to show up at the scheduled time, friends made a report to the police station.

Yesterday evening, S pt. Keith and others ent in search of the missing teenagers in the Macqueripe and Diego Martin areas, but were unsuccessful.

Lost in the Hills

Lost in the Hills by Petra Pierre © 1985

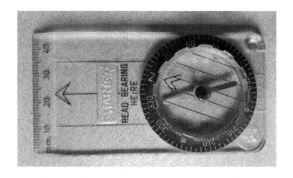

The road of life is sometimes smooth,
And sometimes fraught with danger;
But if you have God as your guide,
No doubts or fears will linger.

The journey started full of fun,
No thoughts of danger present.
Delight was clear on everyone,
The faces bright and radiant.

But suddenly, from down below,
A gloomy cry was sounded.
The road we're taking we must not go,
We are not homeward bounded.

Lost in the Hills

Who cares, we still had hopes to reach
Our destiny by midday.
We had two hours again to spare,
Let's find another pathway!

We did find one and it seemed right;
Our hope began to flutter.
But at the top, what a dreadful sight!
There was no sign that home was nearer.

Depression settled, hope was gone;
There's no way out, we're stalled.
Time was slipping away so quickly,
Would we make it home at all?

So deep were we in our despair,
All hopes of home were dim
But then, Oh yes, *let's say a prayer,*
But first we'll sing a hymn.

Petra Pierre - Robertson

We did, trust me, it felt great;
No more obstacles we thought.
After all, we did have faith
That God would bring us out.

But God knew that deep down inside
Our hearts lay doubts and fears.
He knew that even though we prayed,
We still were close to tears.

Answer our prayers He certainly did,
But His response was wait.
He delayed our exit from the trap of hills
Until we had sufficient faith.

So wait we did, upon a log,
With no food, no clothes, no shelter.
But we relied upon the Lord,
And our faith grew a little stronger.

Lost in the Hills

The place was dark, the log was cold,
And though our stomachs rumbled,
We knew the Lord was in control,
And He our spirits humbled.

The next day on our journey down,
We often met with danger.
But this time around instead of gloom,
Our faith made things seem brighter.

We all agreed vehemently,
That God brought us out safely.
If you don't believe, you take a trek
Through those hills where we made that journey.

Also by Petra Pierre – Robertson

"No Guarantee"

Cynical Darcy ran from relationships and had no intention of ever getting married. Trying to hide from an annoying suitor Jared, she accidentally bumped into a stranger, Mario, who saved her from an undignified and embarrassing fall on the crowded pavement of St. Jean, the capital city. In her ongoing attempt to avoid Jared, she pretended to be in a relationship with Mario. Because Mario was a visitor to the island she felt that the chances of their seeing each other again were nil. As fate would have it however, they did see each other again...

"The Uncontrollable Flame"

On the brink of marriage and newly converted, Shannon gave up Josh – a nonbeliever – for Christ, decrying physical attraction in the process. Timmy, an on and off Christian for whom she has absolutely no physical attraction, seems a safe option years after her break-up with Josh. Then Phil arrives on the scene, messing with her safe formula and destabilizing her equilibrium in ways Josh never did and Timmy never could!

"Second Chances"

Dalere's secure and comfortable life is shattered by a tragic family event. Violently abused, she flees the drunken wrath of a relative. She is almost taken hostage but for the timely intervention of a curious stranger who gets involved on encountering her desperate flight from attackers. This accidental meeting ultimately provides a second chance that neither of them could have predicted.

Made in the USA
Columbia, SC
11 June 2025